Identity and Data Protection
for the Average Person

Written by:
Michael Pasono
Volume 1 – Revision 3 - 2024

Contents

Overview 4

   About the Author 4

   Why Important 6

      Companies 7

      Hackers 8

      Manipulation 10

      How to protect yourself 11

   Further reference 12

Chapter 1 - Understanding Free vs Paid Business Model 13

   Two Models 13

      Free Model 14

      Paid Model 15

Chapter 2 - Internet Browsing 16

   Web Search Engines (What you search for) 16

   Anonymous Browser (What your location is) 19

   Virtual Private Networks (VPN) 21

Chapter 3 - Cell Phones 24

   Google's Android vs Apple iOS 24

   Cloud and Backups 28

Chapter 4 - Passwords 30

   Best Practices 30

   Multi-factor Authentication 32

   Software Tools 33

Chapter 5 - Email Addresses 34

Best Practices 34

Chapter 6 - Computer Protection 36

Anti-Virus and Malware 36

Firewall 37

Chapter 7 - Software Updates 38

Best Practices 38

Chapter 8 - Social Hacking 39

Phishing and Clickbait 39

Domain Registration 41

Chapter 9 - Removing your digital data footprint 42

Directory Listings 42

Social Media 44

Companies 45

Chapter 10 – Preventing Identity Loss 46

Credit Bureaus 46

Conclusion 47

Overview

About the Author

Michael Pasono, CISSP is the author behind *Identity and Data Protection for the Average Person* which underscores the importance of protecting your personal identity and data as technology and data collection methods advance.

Michael's professional experience and advocacy in systems quality improvement, cybersecurity, and data protection has him recognized as an industry leader in researching technology innovations and assuring high quality systems.

Michael shares key threats and recommends approaches to protect your identity and data for the average person. The recommendations are provided by Michael and not any paid sponsors or partners.

Why Important

As data collection methods have advanced rapidly over the last decade, more personal information is being collected and stored somewhere in data centers and more recently in the cloud. Even stored multiple times for multiple people or purposes. Threat actors and data collection companies are using programs written specifically to scour the Internet and build profiles of people.

There are 3 main attacks on your personal information with you not realizing it. I will break down 3 key areas and why your understanding is just as important as in how to stop it.

Companies

Companies are capitalizing on collecting as much data as they can about their potential and current customers and it's beginning to shine a light into data privacy rights for the average person. With companies collecting so much data, they must hire security experts to keep this data safe to assure their brand reputation. Companies do this collection because they realize your data turns into revenue for them and shareholders. [OBJ]

Hackers

Not only have companies realized this potential revenue source in collecting data but hackers are also realizing this to extort it for capital gains. The two highest paying industries for hackers right now are Healthcare and Financial records as these companies typically have enough data on one individual to initiate identity theft and/or potentially blackmail important people. Individual personal records can fetch well over $1,000-$2,000 on the black market (aka Dark Web) and some databases have millions of records...you can do the math.

Manipulation

Along with data collection for capital gains; it is important to understand how it is impacting society today. Data can be used to manipulate people on social media and news outlets as computer systems can target political ideals which you might be on the fence on. As more data is collected on you, more predictions can be made on you and even persuade you to act in a particular way. [OBJ]

How to protect yourself

The average person is being attacked on three main fronts; Company data collecting, black market hackers, and social manipulation. This book was written to help you combat these attacks. You should be following a zero-trust policy allowing only what data is minimally required to use a product or service you would like to use. If you feel too much of your personal information is being collected when signing up or purchasing, you should look for a replacement and stop or boycott that company.

Further reference

The creation of this book is in partnership with Apply QA, LLC; a leading provider of best practices and consultation services for software quality assurance best practices. In fact, the founder and CEO of this company is Michael himself.

Please visit https://www.applyqa.com to check out their educational products and services.

Chapter 1 - Understanding Free vs Paid Business Model

Two Models

This chapter is probably one of the most important concepts that I would like you to take away from this book. This has the highest impact decision that allows you to justify if you should use a particular company product or service based on how data is leveraged or stored. Understanding the business model of free vs paid, this chapter explains 2 main models for how businesses attract potential customers and earn revenue. This will help you make the correct lifestyle decisions to protect your identity and data.

Free Model

At a very high level, free business models provide their customers free access to their products or services in **exchange** for something. Typically, this exchange is for the customers' rights to use their data as they see fit. This business model is what the technology industry leverages the most, especially for new start-ups that do not have a lot of capital and are looking to gain customers quickly.

As these companies mature, these free models could convert over some type of pay-for-service model but if that happens; you have already agreed to provide more of your data from the beginning. If you ever want to see the type of data a particular company collects, ask or view their privacy policy. Privacy policies are typically published on the company website, and some are in a hard-to-find place. Begin to pay closer attention to what you agree to give up using any product or service.

Paid Model

Regarding using paid services, it's a little better regarding data collection. These companies will still collect your data, but their main use is not to generate revenue but still leveraged as another avenue to generate future revenue or improve customer experience. Regarding the type of data being collected it can be as simple as your email and basic demographics to advanced website tracking, knowing exactly how much time you spent on a particular webpage or tracking the clicking on what interests you.

Chapter 2 - Internet Browsing

Web Search Engines
(What you search for)

Everyday millions of people go to search engines to search for something they want more information on. Little did you know that most of your search words are tracked. That level of tracking is dependent on which service you are using.

For example, if you are using Google, you might already be signed-in using one of their services such as Gmail to check your emails and decide to search for something to buy for your relative. When you stay sign-ed in, this gives Google the right to track your activity within their ecosystem of products. When you search for gifts within Google, it will show you any of their products that they might sell first, then their ad sponsors, and then regular listings.

What Google can do with this information is quite powerful. For example, they know you are looking for a gift around a particular timeframe, which can then send you reminders next year to purchase again.

You can see that making a simple search can turn into an elaborate attempt to persuade you into purchasing from them or a sponsor again. Google can then take this data and sell it to third parties that may target your interests for additional revenue.

To combat this detailed search tracking, I recommend a couple approaches.

1) If you must use a popular search engine, make sure you sign-out of your account and delete your browser cache/temporary internet files, then close your browser and reopen it. This might not fully block all data from being tracked but helps limit your exposure if you must use that service.

Unfortunately, this process needs to be repeated frequently and you must keep a close eye on if you are still logged in.

2) Set a non-tracking web browser as your default. You can do this in the settings of your web browser or mobile phone. I would recommend using a service such as DuckDuckGo which doesn't track your personal data to execute searches.

Anonymous Browser
(What your location is)

Using an anonymous browser is a good approach to limit your identity and data tracking attempts. Anonymous browsers focus more on your location vs. what items you might be searching for. Anonymous browsers are built with the concept of protecting your identity and location in mind. There are 2 different types of related anonymous browsers you can use to help protect what you are searching for tracking purposes.

1) Anonymous Web Surfing gives you a portal to connect to another website from the anonymous website. What this does is block your IP address from being known to the new website you want to visit. Think of it as a website hop and your activity is being routed in between your physical PC to a middleman (anonymous web surfing) to new website.

2) Tor Application Web Browser takes location privacy to another level. This is an actual browser that you download, and it will connect to multiple locations to make location tracing nearly impossible. The only downside to this is there is typically a speed reduction due to all the data being passed in between the different locations and back to your PC.

Virtual Private Networks (VPN)

Using a virtual private network allows you to hide the data and your location that your computer is sending to whatever website you are visiting. This is used to make sure no hackers can intercept your data in let's say a public WIFI space. Most companies use this VPN technology to allow their workers to maybe work from home.

To setup a VPN it typically requires either a physical box or software to be installed on your pc to connect securely. If you are to leverage a VPN, please stay away from free services as they tend to be less secure, and your data might still be logged and tracked. Focus on VPN companies that advertise they do not log your activity. You can typically select which state or region you would like to connect to. This is important because if you do not use a VPN, whatever website you visit will get your IP address which can give companies your physical location area such as your Internet Service Provider (ISP). While it might not seem too important if companies know your ISP, it does give attackers more information on what services you use and setup for more targeted attack.

My recommendation is two-fold here, sign-up and set up a virtual private network and use a service that doesn't track your browsing such as DuckDuckGo. This would protect the tracking of your data and your physical location. If you are really looking to block tracking, you could use Tor browser along with a VPN, just make sure you are on a fast connection.

Chapter 3 - Cell Phones

Google's Android vs Apple iOS

Leveraging a cellphone today is a necessity, children are being practically raised on a cellphone and tablets at an alarming rate. Identity and data protection are very important for children and even more so the younger they start. The younger the children are, perform actions such as browsing YouTube or downloading apps that allow companies to build persona's and target them for future purchases throughout their life, even could manipulate them. This puts a lot of pressure on the parents to make sure they are setting up their devices with the correct privacy settings.

This brings up an interesting topic I get asked a lot about, which cellphone platform should I use to limit my exposure. About 10 years ago I would say it's personal preference as many of those in the tech industry lean towards Android due to newer features being rolled out but now it is a different story. The way Android updates its software is not consistent compared to let's say iOS. To reduce any threats of being hacked, companies need to patch their software quickly. Android phones do not all get the same updates nor at the same time. This leaves Android phones more valuable to attackers leveraging older exploits.

Android was built on Google's ecosystem and the business model is a free to use model. Which again, if you read my earlier chapter on free vs paid business model, you see that more of your activity is being logged and tracked to compensate for getting something for free. Converting your actions from let's say a PC over to cellphone or tablet allows for greater integration of free services and ease of use which also allows more data to be easily shared back to the platform or app companies. This makes it difficult for the average user to stop the tracking.

iOS was built on Apple's ecosystem and the business model is a bit different. You pay for most services you want to use. I'm not saying Apple is not tracking some of your information, but they are collecting less. iOS leaps ahead of Android regarding data protection and clearly stating their privacy policy. Regarding patching security exploits, Apple controls its hardware and software and can roll out updates to all the supported devices at once. This is critical for data protection because it lessens the number of exploits that can be used to gather your personal information.

Regarding identity and data protection, my recommendation is the following if you are using either Android or iOS. If you must use Android device, make sure you pay more attention to the type of data that is being logged and shared with. If you have a child using an Android device, make sure you set up FamilyLink application which allows parents more control on the actions they might perform. This will limit some unneeded sharing of personal data. Overall, I recommend leveraging Apple devices and their ecosystem due to its enhanced practice on keeping its devices updated consistently and the future software updates that are coming to iOS. The latest version of iOS will be scanning applications and notifying you of potential data sharing that you might not want to happen.

Cloud and Backups

As more data is moving to the cloud at an alarming rate to bring information on demand to mobile devices; this brings more attention to the fact that company's data is leaving their own data centers over to someone else's and typically in a public cloud setting. Attackers are targeting more cloud service providers and those configurations due to newer technology and potentially more holes yet to be patched. As any company moves to the cloud, they typically copy data as a backup in case any issues occur. This data is usually stored in a database with different levels of encryption for when it's at rest or in motion.

As the average person uses a company service, their data is in the hands of many folks and replicated for many internal uses that you might not be aware of. These uses can be from database backups to software development, or even testing new features. It is important to continue to follow the recommendations in the book to limit your exposure to data you are giving away.

Regarding personal device backups such as your phone or tablet, if you can encrypt your backup instance, please do so as it adds another layer of security if your PC or a particular company gets breached.

Chapter 4 - Passwords

Best Practices

There are many books written just on securing passwords and different types of encryptions. The message I want to provide is don't over think this. Follow these simple best practices for creating your password in your everyday life.

1) Do not use the same password for multiple sites
2) Use a combination of letters, upper/lower case, numbers, and characters. The longer the better.
3) Do not use any personal names or pet names
4) Avoid higher level names (i.e. God, goddess, admin, sysadmin, secret)
5) Change your password if the company gets a data breach
6) Change your password every 3-6 months

Multi-factor Authentication

The use of multi-factor authentication has really been the gold standard in taking password protection to the next level. The concept is simple, to login to a product or service you must have 2 methods of authentication. Typically, this is your password and a text or email with a code to login. More advanced systems could also include biometrics such as fingerprints or eye scanners. It is recommended to enable multi-factor authentication on all the companies you do share personal information or do business with.

Software Tools

Over the last few years password managers and vaults have been created to help everyday people manage all the complex passwords they have since every company wants some authentication and personalization. Some browser companies offer some ease of use by asking if you want to store your username and password. I do not recommend storing these credentials in any browser, especially if you are using a public PC. On your personal PC or mobile it is recommended to use a leading password manager or vault with a very secure password. You also don't want to leave it in plain sight. Think of your password manager's password and the keys to the bank, so keep it hidden.

Chapter 5 - Email Addresses

Best Practices

Something as innocent as sharing an email address to any company is safe, right? It should be given caution, choosing your email provider and what your actual address name is can make a difference to protect your identity and data. Again, using a free service will likely allow the email provider to scan your emails and sell your interests to third parties.

If you are technically savvy, I would recommend setting up a website domain and adding an email service to it. It is not free, but you then have more control of how your email data is being processed. If you must use a free email service, I would recommend you use an email address that doesn't identify your name and/or include any personal dates (i.e. Birth year, age, location). Also review their privacy policy around their email service to see if you are willing to sign-up.

Chapter 6 - Computer Protection

Anti-Virus and Malware

Over the last 40 years anti-virus tools have been recommended to help protect your pc or mobile device from being infected with a virus. There are different types of viruses, but most will slow down your PC, disable it, and/or log keystrokes. While it's important to use anti-virus software, advances in operating system defenses and update speed have made the need to purchase less needed. If you want to purchase a third-party anti-virus, make sure it's a paid service and not a free service. Some free anti-virus programs can cause more harm than good, installing bloatware and trying to sell you more products you don't need. I do recommend having a good malware protection program on top of standard operating system defenses built in.

Firewall

A firewall is a way for your network or pc to block connections between different applications or ports. As a best practice, it's recommended to disable all ports and only open the applications or ports needed. If a virus does get installed on your PC, your firewall will likely block the data being passed between your infected PC and the person that created the virus, limiting the damage you could experience later.

Chapter 7 - Software Updates

Best Practices

The majority of applications and operating systems have software updates to improve performance and security of new exploits. It is advised to allow automatic updates to these software updates to occur to reduce any delay in patching. A delay in patching allows more time for attackers to steal your personal data. Also avoid letting anyone know if you are running any old versions of operating systems or applications. Telling someone you are still using an old version of Microsoft Windows can open you up to a potential theft of your data.

Chapter 8 - Social Hacking

Phishing and Clickbait

The rise of everyone using social media platforms to stay connected and current have given attackers other avenues to gather data from you. Using any public social media posts and phishing attempts, attackers can target you to get you to click on a link which might infect your PC or mobile device. This is one of the most popular attack methods being used on average person. I recommend you be very cautious about who you are and what information you are sharing on any social media site that is public. You should never list any personal information or location information. This is a newer concept for the average person to understand.

What makes phishing so effective is the attacker will use information on people you know or services you use gathered from public information. Other signs you can tell you might be phished are bad grammar, invalid website addresses, or invalid website syntax. If you get an email asking for any SSN or Credit Card/Bank info with a sense of urgency, that is a big red flag to immediately delete and do not click on anything. Companies will not ask for this information via email, if they do and you think it's valid, call them first and provide over phone vs sending it in email.

Domain Registration

To create a website for business or personal use, you typically search for a domain name to use. It is critical that whenever you purchase a domain, I can't stress this enough that you should purchase the domain privacy option. If an attacker wanted to find out any physical address of a domain or person, they can do this very easily by performing a lookup on a domain name. So, if they leveraged public social media and domain register information, they could then leverage for future attacks to gain access to your personal data.

Chapter 9 - Removing your digital data footprint

Directory Listings

Remember the big physical phone books delivered to your house? It listed every person and business in your city. Along with your name, it provided your addresses and phone number. With the invention of the internet, these phone books have gone digital too. The good thing here is most of these directory listings must legally provide a way to protect or remove your name on request. They are typically at the bottom of the webpage.

There are also paid services that will search the internet for your information and submit requests on your behalf to remove. These are not failproof as the internet is large and not all websites are indexed in search engines. If you submit a request to remove your information, there is typically a 1–2-week turnaround per website. You also must remember that some search engines cache websites which could potentially still show your information for longer.

Social Media

As more social media platforms are built, the average person only needs two at the most unless you are a business or an influencer. You need one to stay connected for your career and one for family and friends. If you switch your main social media platform, remember to close out your old one and request data to be removed from their system. For the social media platform, you are using, make it a practice to remove old or outdated information especially if it is public.

Companies

As data privacy laws are advancing for consumer rights, many companies will have to provide their customers with a way to remove their personal data on request. This is more relevant in Europe and GDPR regulations but expanding rapidly globally. If you no longer are using a product or service, it is recommended to reach out to the company to have your account deactivated and/or removed. Your proactive approach to having old accounts removed could save you from a potential breach down the road.

Chapter 10 – Preventing Identity Loss

Credit Bureaus

It is a given that your data will be part of some data breach. It is just a matter of time. To combat this, it is recommended to check your credit report every couple of months. If you have been notified of a data breach with your information, you can reach out to a credit bureau to put a verification lock or a hard freeze on your account. The verification lock is a good next step to take because it still allows you to leverage your credit but requires the loan giver to personally call you to verify. If you have already had your identity stolen, you likely have hard freeze in place until more time passes.

Conclusion

With the advancement in data collection techniques and bots scanning the internet, along with artificial intelligence machines connecting multiple datasets to make sense of the data, it is important to understand how much personal and tracking data you are allowing these businesses to collect on you.

Information security best practice is to follow zero-trust method which can be transferred from enterprise for the average person as a best practice. Begin by restricting everything and gradually granting more permissions. If you have already signed up for every free service in the world, I would suggest backtracking and starting to remove those permissions or putting in requests to deactivate accounts no longer being used.

Once you start reading more of the privacy policies and permissions needed upfront, you will recognize what data you could potentially be sharing, and the risks associated.

My hope is that you get some new insight into why your data is being sought after and what approaches you can take to avoid being a victim of identity theft or data theft.